The Fabian Society

The Fabian Society is Britain's oldest political think tank. Since 1884 the Society has played a central role in developing political ideas and public policy on the left.

Through a wide range of publications and events the Society influences political and public thinking, but also provides a space for broad and open-minded debate, drawing on an unrivalled external network and its own expert research and analysis.

The Society is alone among think tanks in being a democratically-constituted membership organisation, with almost 7,000 members. During its history the membership has included many of the key thinkers on the British left and every Labour Prime Minister. Today it counts over 200 parliamentarians in its number. Member-led activity includes 70 local Fabian societies, the Scottish and Welsh Fabians, the Fabian Women's Network and the Young Fabians, which is itself the leading organisation on the left for young people to debate and influence political ideas.

The Society was one of the original founders of the Labour Party and is constitutionally affiliated to the party. It is however editorially, organisationally and financially independent and works with a wide range of partners of all political persuasions and none.

www.fabians.org.uk.

Joining the Fabians is easy
For more information about joining the Fabian Society and to learn more about our recent publications, please turn to the final page.

FEPS is the first progressive political foundation established at the European level. Created in 2007 and co-financed by the European Parliament, it aims at establishing an intellectual crossroad between social democracy and the European project. It puts fresh thinking at the core of its action and serves as an instrument for pan-European intellectual and political reflection.

Acting as a platform for ideas, FEPS relies first and foremost on a network of members composed of more than 58 national political foundations and think tanks from all over the EU. The Foundation also closely collaborates with a number of international correspondents and partners in the world that share the ambition to foster research, promote debate and spread the progressive thinking.

www.feps-europe.eu

You can also find FEPS on

🕸 Facebook
🕸 Twitter
🕸 Netvibes

FOUNDATION FOR EUROPEAN
PROGRESSIVE STUDIES
FONDATION EUROPÉENNE
D'ÉTUDES PROGRESSISTES

BACK TO EARTH

Reconnecting people and politics

Edited by Ed Wallis and Ania Skrzypek-Claassens

FOUNDATION FOR EUROPEAN
PROGRESSIVE STUDIES
FONDATION EUROPÉENNE
D'ÉTUDES PROGRESSISTES

Fabian Society
61 Petty France
London SW1H 9EU
www.fabians.org.uk

   Head of Editorial: Ed Wallis
   Editorial Assistant: Anya Pearson

Foundation for European Progressive Studies
Rue Montoyer 40
1000 Brussels, Belgium
www.feps-europe.eu

   Senior Research Fellow: Ania Skrzypek-Claassens

A FEPS / Fabian book
First published 2014
ISBN 978-0-7163-4122-2

Printed and bound by DG3

British Library Cataloguing in Publication data.
A catalogue record for this book is available from
the British Library.

CONTENTS

CONTRIBUTORS

Jenny Andersson is CNRS senior research fellow in the Centre d'Etudes Européennes, Sciences Po, Paris

David Bailey is a lecturer at the Department of Political Science and International Studies at the University of Birmingham and a member of the FEPS Next Left Working Group.

Alan Finlayson is professor of political and social theory at the University of East Anglia

Katie Ghose is chief executive of the Electoral Reform Society

Cordelia Hay is research lead at BritainThinks

David Lammy is Labour MP for Tottenham

Deborah Mattinson is founder director at BritainThinks

Baroness Royall is Labour's leader in the House of Lords and a vice president of the Party of European Socialists (PES)

Ania Skrzypek-Claassens is senior research fellow at the Foundation for European Progressive Studies (FEPS)

Stephen Twigg is shadow minister for political and constitutional reform

Ed Wallis is head of editorial at the Fabian Society

Jon Wilson teaches history at King's College London and wrote the Fabian pamphlet *Letting Go: How Labour can learn to stop worrying and trust the people*

FOREWORD

Stephen Twigg MP

We are facing a democratic deficit of startling proportions. Across Europe, electoral turnout has
been on a downward trend for decades and
membership of a political party is dwindling compared to
the post-war era. In the UK, only 44 per cent of those aged
18–24 voted in 2010 and a recent survey found that only a
third of 16–24 year olds say they have an interest in politics.

The challenge of confronting our ailing democracy is
vast. The research undertaken for this pamphlet emphasises the importance of the challenge and underlines the
deep disconnect between the public and politics. The
verdict of participants in the democratic deficit workshop
organised by BritainThinks was predictably damning:
politicians don't seem representative of the communities
they serve and don't speak in a language many can relate
to. They want politicians to work harder to listen and to
interact with their communities and act on principle and
not simply chase short-term popularity.

Politicians must accept this problem before we can
solve it. There may be a temptation to retreat from political
reform, especially in the midst of the significant economic
and social challenges we face. The next Labour government
will take a different approach and open up our democracy
to bring about change. It is not enough to do nothing and
hope the tide changes. It is essential that we seek to explore

new ways of achieving democratic renewal and political reform.

This research offers a sense of direction for Labour party policy. It was no surprise that a policy of decentralising power and giving communities more say over local decision making was popular in the 'Dragons' Den' workshop, where citizens took the part of the Dragons. As the late congressman, Tip O'Neill, once said, "all politics is local". Purposeful political engagement will only come through empowering people to make the decisions that affect their community. Ed Miliband has already called for a new era of public services, to put the power in the hands of parents, patients and public service users. Labour recognises that a centrally-controlled Whitehall machine is old fashioned and not fit for purpose in the 21st century.

The Dragons' Den did not always agree with Labour policy. Ed Miliband has announced that the next Labour government will introduce votes at the age of 16. Introducing votes at 16 is a bold and radical proposal that, if implemented with care, has the potential to energise a new generation of politically active and engaged citizens. The Dragons suggested that younger people are already severely disengaged from politics and unlikely to take up the opportunity to vote.

I share the Citizen-Dragons' concerns that lowering the voting age should not be taken in isolation. Votes at 16 must go hand-in-hand with wider youth engagement and a renewed commitment to citizenship education. Over time, voting and political debate could become a rite of passage in our education system, like taking exams. The last Labour government made great strides with its introduction of citizenship as a subject in secondary school. Citizenship education should sit at the core of our curriculum, giving young people an understanding, deeper knowledge and interest in civic issues. Votes at 16 would place renewed emphasis on this.

Instead of legislating to lower the voting age, the Dragons suggested politicians should visit schools to engage in political debate, to educate young voters. From Loughborough to Brighton, Ealing to Barrow, I have been doing just this, asking students their views and opinions on politics and the issue of votes at 16 specifically.

I have found that youth is by no means automatically linked to apathy, and the reasons behind low turnout are multi-faceted and complicated. Young people today are often highly political but understandably wary of formal party politics. Many don't feel politicians are listening to their concerns or talking about their aspirations. Opening up our democratic system to younger people is an important way in which we can solve this problem. Rather than turn our backs, we must instead seek to address the current democratic malaise by empowering young people.

As well as lowering the voting age, Labour is developing policies across the political reform agenda. We want to make it easier for people to register and vote at elections, and are looking at radical changes to achieve this. To reform the government's gagging law, we are consulting widely with charities and campaigners to build a regulatory framework which protects freedom of speech but ensures accountability. Labour remains committed to a democratically elected second chamber. There is still a lot to do, but Labour is beginning to create a wide ranging reform programme.

The Fabians, FEPS and BritainThinks have adopted the correct approach by putting the citizen at the heart of building a new policy programme. We all need to listen a lot more if we are going to close the democratic deficit. This research is a welcome contribution to this process. Labour is listening in opposition, and will achieve real change in government.

INTRODUCTION

Ed Wallis

Why don't people trust politicians? This is a question we confront with increasing urgency in political debate across Europe. Poll after poll tells of the declining esteem in which our political leaders are held, and the forthcoming European elections look set to be a new low-water mark for democratic engagement. However, this pamphlet shows that perhaps the more pertinent concern is: why don't politicians trust people?

New, deliberative work conducted for this pamphlet by BritainThinks brought together 15 members of the electorate – half of whom were swing voters, and half non-voters – to understand people's gut instincts about politics and the growing antipathy towards the political class, and to work together on some solutions. 'Politicians who are more like one of us', 'politicians who listen to people', and 'politics that makes people feel like they have an impact' were the common refrains. BritainThinks report that

> *"When asked what they'd most like to change about politics, almost every non-voter or swing voter in the room talked about changing politicians themselves: who they are, the way that they talk and act, and the kinds of issues they prioritise."*

As Baroness Royall points out in chapter eight, across Europe "politics is viewed by many as a game played by a small elite, with the great majority of people neither able nor welcome to join in."

This echoes previous work on political disengagement, both by FEPS (see vol. 7 of the FEPS Next Left Books Series) and a Fabian Society poll conducted by YouGov in 2012, which found that voters and non-voters alike had not given up entirely on democracy, but wanted a political culture that is less adversarial, less distant and more in tune with real life. This poses a quandary for political reformers, whose methods have tended to focus on constitutional changes to make politics more open and democratic. If the essence of the problem is cultural – who politicians are and how they act – can mechanical solutions really make much difference? There are undoubtedly some things. As Katie Ghose notes in chapter three, structural changes "would themselves make a big difference in the way our politicians behaved – and the way the public engages with politics … We need to commit to a wide range of reforms that target both the structure of our politics and the culture of those participating". And measures to ensure that political candidates were drawn from a wider range of life experience than professional politics would make the democratic process feel less like a game being played for the amusement of a privileged few. But, as Ania Skrzypek-Claassens notes when surveying the even greater political disconnection that exists at the European level in chapter seven, "this is about the quality of politics, not about institutional change. The solution to political disengagement with the European Union is not a new treaty."

The big change we need to make is in how we think about power. In our workshop, when people talked about 'politics', they did so exclusively within a parliamentary frame and almost entirely saw politics as something politicians did. Everything was national and passive. However, when we discussed how to fix things, the solutions people were excited about were local and active. People in our workshop were overwhelmingly positive – often moved – about having the power to change their own community themselves. 'Giving power to local communities' was far and away the most popular of various pitches to improve politics.

But there is an ambiguity in how people perceive localism. Our 2012 YouGov poll found the main thing that would make non-voters more likely to vote at the next election would be 'if people in political parties spent less time trying to win my vote and more time doing good work in my neighbourhood'. This was supported by 25 per cent of respondents, compared to just 2 per cent who said they'd be more likely to vote if 'a party official knocked on my door to discuss political issues, or I received a telephone call or a letter'. Yet while participants in our workshop were attracted by this idea of community organising, where people come together in their local neighbourhood to act on issues the care about, they didn't really see it as 'politics' and couldn't really conceptualise it making much of a difference. People felt it wouldn't work because power resides elsewhere. So, as BritainThinks explain, to give the idea "greater legitimacy, and crucially, greater impact, citizens proposed the addition of local, issue-based referendums to decide policy and spending priorities." The effect of this amendment is to put an idea which seeks to build a broader notion of democratic empowerment back into an electoral box and return it to how politics is more commonly understood: voting so politicians do things.

But rather than suggesting a lack of appetite for being more actively involved in democracy and a preference to simply let politicians get on with it, perhaps this narrowing of the canvas reflects the limited possibilities of the politics we have been offered. Jon Wilson describes in chapter one the predominant 'Hobbesian' view of political power:

"that citizens give up a proportion of their freedom when they elect political leaders. People keep their freedom to run their private lives as they choose, but hand over their power to shape the place they live to politicians who, from then onwards until the next election, act without the consent or co-operation of those they rule." People are disillusioned with politics, Wilson argues, because this is not the reality of how power works; our elected representatives are not simply able to 'deliver' things on our behalf. If this conception were ever true, it certainly isn't in what Colin Crouch has described as our current 'post-democratic' arrangements, whereby power no longer resides solely within the national polity but is "increasingly being exercised by international business interests ranging at will over transnational territories beyond the reach of nation states". But while power is certainly dispersed globally, it is also dispersed locally, as Wilson argues, "centred in the life of institutions we encounter everyday, in social systems and practices that can't be controlled by legislative force." He concludes that "it's hardly surprising we're turned off by politicians who believe central power can direct things it simply cannot control."

It's worth reviewing complaints about the increasing professionalisation of politics in these terms. Much has been made of our burgeoning 'spadocracy' and the increasing visibility across European political office of former political advisers. Andy Burnham recently said of Britain: "all the current generation of politicians, myself included, typically came up through the back offices. We're the professional politician generation, aren't we?" It's striking to note that not only do all three current party leaders fit this bill, but four of the five candidates for the Labour leadership in 2010 did too. Research by the House of Commons library has shown that it's not necessarily the quantity that is the problem – only around 15 per cent of current MPs fit the mould of 'career politicians'. What matters is that it's the path to power. Recent work by Peter Allen finds that "MPs who worked full-time in politics before being elected dominate the top frontbench positions, whilst colleagues whose political experience consisted of being a local councillor tended to remain backbenchers. Thus, if you a see a politician in the media, chances are they are from the frontbenches, and more likely than not have this type of back-office experience."

But a deeper question about the professionalisation of politics is whether it is, in fact, a profession. What is a profession? It's a type of job that requires special education, training, or skill. For many years, politics was not perceived like this and it was not until the 1960s that what Anthony King famously chronicled as "the rise of the career politician" took hold (coincidentally or not, also when we begin to see steady decline in electoral turnout). The professionalisation of politics suggests power is something that requires professional training to practise, whether that is specific policy expertise, ability to communicate with the media or knowing the corridors of Westminster. However, as Alan Finlayson makes clear in chapter two, the thing politicians actually need to know is what they believe in and why: "a prerequisite for being convincing is having conviction – knowing what your position is, knowing how and why it is different from others' positions and being sure of why you hold it". Political communication needs an argument if it "is to avoid sounding empty, suspicious or indulgent". And the skills politicians really need to have are the ability to bring people together: "to get people in the room by inspiring them with a sense of the possibility of common action" as Jon Wilson puts it.

Underlying this is the need to move on from the view whereby the parliamentary route is the only means of political expression for practitioners and citizens alike. Politics is, in fact, everywhere – yet we tend not to notice it because it's not the way we are used to talking about politics. Marc Stears, a close adviser to Ed Miliband, said when writing about the idea of an 'everyday democracy':

> *"When people think of democracy they often think of the grand political institutions. Their minds go to Westminster or Whitehall, to general elections or constitutional conventions. But the essence of democracy is really much more simple than this. It is found in the relationships – both face-to-face and virtual – that bring individual human beings with different backgrounds, experiences and understandings of their interests, together and transforms them into a collective unit, one capable of common action."*

And so as democratic reformers we need to break out of a purely electoral and constitutional prism. Democracy is a muscle, and restoring it to fitness requires much more regular exercise than just a run around at election time. When we think about democratic reform we need to think about economic democracy, in plural forms of ownership and giving employees a stake in the long-term stewardship of the places they work; we need to think about environmental citizenship, in reinvigorating people's attachment to place and restoring a sense of agency so people can take pride in the communities where they live; we need to think about what Ed Miliband has called "people-powered" public services, so citizens are in charge of their own interactions with the state. As David Lammy writes in chapter four, it's about giving local people the power to prevent "the diversity and fabric of high streets, particularly in deprived areas ... being slowly eroded by a splurge of new betting shops, payday loan companies and pawnbrokers". We need, in short, what GDH Cole termed "the widest possible diffusion of power and responsibility, so as to enlist the active participation of as many as possible of its citizens in the task of democratic self-government".

The left has a special stake in ensuring faith in politics endures. As Tim Horton, David Pinto-Duschinsky, and Jessica Studdert argued in their 2007 Fabian pamphlet *Facing Out*, "a willingness to recognise that others have needs and to accommodate their interests with yours underpins not just democratic politics, but also the legitimacy of the public realm itself." But we tend to think about what this means in practice in a rather reductive way: as sustaining support for social democratic governments, through elections every few years. This is a crucial part of the left's project, but it is not the whole of it. So, as David Bailey, a member of the FEPS Next Left Working Group on Democracy and Euro-parties, writes in chapter six, European social democratic parties need to be much better at accommodating and working with the emerging sources of 'extra-parliamentary' democratic energy that exist outside formal party structures: "Whilst we might have witnessed a decline in popular trust in the political class, this does not necessarily reflect a wider disinterest in politics." And crucially, we need to see democracy spread through all spheres of life. As the BritainThinks research commissioned by FEPS and the Fabian Society for this pamphlet concludes, power needs "to be felt at a local level before people will feel that they have a stake nationally".

Making this leap requires trust, because only by giving it away can politicians win it back.

RESEARCH FINDINGS

Cordelia Hay and Deborah Mattinson

'I want politicians to have firmer ideas, rather than going for ideas to get elected.'

'I want politicians to be more responsive to the public good, not to lobbyists.'

'I'd like politicians to spend more time in their constituencies, with fewer perks and less taking advantage.'

'I want less nepotism. I'd like everyone to feel that they could be in politics.'

With public trust in politicians to tell the truth at a paltry 18 per cent[1] and turnout at UK local elections hovering at just above 30 per cent on average across 2012, the democratic deficit has never felt so real.

That's why we designed a unique project with the Fabian Society and FEPS setting out to understand the problem and, crucially, to identify citizen-shaped solutions by bringing together 15 members of the electorate for a 'co-creative' workshop. The scene was set as a Dragons' Den, with citizens taking the part of Dragons, and four political campaigners and activists – the political 'entrepreneurs' – whose pitches to improve politics were under scrutiny.

The workshop programme:

- **The problem:** After introductions, we asked citizens what's wrong with politics today, and what they'd most like to change about it.
- **The solutions:** The four political 'entrepreneurs' then each pitched their idea for improving politics, followed by a grilling from the Dragons (or citizens).
- **The citizen-improved solutions:** At this point, our Dragons' Den diverged from its namesake as the tables were turned back on citizens to work co-creatively alongside the political entrepreneurs to develop their ideas to improve politics, and throw new ideas into the mix. The end result was a shortlist of refined, 'citizen-proofed' ideas.

Our Dragons were drawn from across Greater London, and represented a cross-section of society in terms of gender, age, ethnicity and socioeconomic background. They included an equal mix of non-voters and swing voters, who rated their feelings about politics today at on average just 3.5 on a 10-point scale, where 10 is very positive and 0 is very negative.

They included:

- Bob, a 65-year-old pensioner from Greenwich who follows current affairs avidly but hasn't felt able to vote for any of the main political parties for years. He is deeply sceptical that politics is going to change any time soon.

- Dionne, a mother in her late 20s from Tottenham who has a public sector office job. She likes the idea of getting involved locally, but her faith in people power has been badly dented after a failed attempt by her local community to stop the closure of a hospital ward.

- Aidan, 37, lives in Ealing with his partner and teenage children and works in security at an airport. Although he often tells his children that they should take more of an interest in the world around them, he himself feels that politics factors low down on his list of priorities. Besides, he says, 'politicians are more likely to listen to lobbyists than they are to me'.

The problem: Why do so many citizens feel disconnected from politics and decision-making?

We began by asking each of our Dragons to identify the one thing that they'd most like to change about politics. Their responses were strikingly similar, and centred around aspirations for:

- **'Politicians who are more like one of us'**, who win their place in politics on their own merit, and who speak in plain English rather than PMQ-style squabbling or spin

  "Politics always seemed a bit like it was for someone else. They need to make it easier for me to understand – a bit less complicated."

- **'Politicians who listen to people'**, symbolised by politicians who spend more time in their constituencies, and opportunities for voters to quiz politicians on the issues that matter

  "I want to see more interaction with ordinary people. I loved those live debates."

- **'Politics that makes people feel like they have an impact'** and incentivises them to take the time to vote

"They need to give us the feeling that we genuinely get to have a say on things like education and health."

- **'Politics that is led by issues, rather than people and parties'**, with ideas borne out of sound principles, not quick wins

  "I'd most like to see parties with a positive agenda, that try to lead and convince the electorate, not pandering to it to find the most popular consensus."

With strong agreement in the room that change was urgently needed, we asked our Dragons what would make an idea to improve politics 'successful' in their eyes. They deliberated a number of factors, with common themes surrounding ideas that involve ordinary people, that make people feel more connected to politics, that respond to citizen-led demands rather than political agendas, and where the impact of the change can be seen and felt, rather than simply talked about.

The solution: Ideas for re-engaging voters with politics

Next, the political 'entrepreneurs' (four political campaigners and activists) were up against our Dragons, each pitching their idea to improve politics. After giving each idea an initial grilling in the Den, the Dragons resumed their role as citizens, working alongside the entrepreneurs to improve and 'citizen-proof' each idea. Notably, they also added their own idea into the mix: stricter rules to govern MPs. Here are the results:

Idea 1: Taking action to engage younger people in politics

The original pitch: Katie Ghose (Electoral Reform Society) proposed that votes should be introduced for 16 and 17 year olds to engage citizens in the democratic process as early as possible.

What worked well: The Dragons agreed that it is critically important that politicians make the effort to engage younger people to guarantee future generations of interested, active voters.

What worked less well: However, this idea was felt to be one step ahead of where younger people are today – severely disengaged from politics and very unlikely to take up the opportunity to vote. Aidan put it as: *"The only way they'd vote is if you gave them each a Playstation."*

The improved idea: Based on the principle that younger people need a *reason* to vote before they are given the right to vote, citizens proposed that the idea be improved by:

- Potential and elected candidates going in to local schools to speak to teenagers, with Question Time style debates
- Information and education for younger people in school and through the media about how politics impacts on real life
- A birthday letter from the Queen when you hit voting age to remind you about your new right to vote
- Politics that features policies that are clearly relevant to younger people, for example surrounding apprenticeships and internships

Idea 2: Stricter systems to hold MPs to account

The original pitch: Mark Ferguson (Labour List) pitched for a system to recall MPs who weren't felt to be adequately representing their constituents.

What worked well: The idea was felt to draw on the right principle of holding MPs to account, and ensuring that they don't feel able to take advantage of the system.

What works less well: The Dragons were concerned that the idea would be difficult to implement in practice, and made the point that voters can already hold MPs to account by not re-electing them.

The improved idea: Citizens proposed instead that a local governing body should be set up in each constituency immediately following a general election, operating according to a jury service style system. The MP would be required to report to the governing body on a monthly basis, and the body would have the authority to decide whether or not the MP was fulfilling his or her promises and job requirements.

Idea 3: Decentralising power and giving communities more say over local decision making

The original idea: Rowenna Davis (PPC for Southampton Itchen) called for devolving more national decisions to a local level, drawing on the example of local councils being unable to deny planning permission for betting shops on the high street.

What worked well: The Dragons were compelled by Rowenna Davis' first-hand experiences of trying to effect change at a local level in Peckham, and many agreed that local communities do not have enough of a say over what happens in their local area.

What worked less well: Some questioned whether local councils are any more trustworthy or effective than national politicians.

The improved idea: Citizens felt it was critical that communities as well as local councils should have a say over local decisions, suggesting that the idea could be improved by:

- Ensuring that a certain amount of funding is allocated to local community groups who want to bring positive change to the local area
- Guaranteeing that a certain percentage of council tax goes towards spending on the local area, and that spending priorities are decided (or at least informed) by local people
- Operating according to a credit union type system, to ensure that local people know and have a say over where their money (council tax) is going

Idea 4: Community organising backed up by local referendums

The original idea: Marcus Roberts (Fabian Society) spoke out for community organising, allowing politicians and the public to share the responsibility of bringing about local change.

What worked well: Dragons reacted positively to the idea that community organising would require MPs to spend a certain amount of time in their constituency, and to work closely and collaboratively with their constituents. The pitch also chimed with the Dragons' own arguments that a successful idea to improve politics should involve 'ordinary' people, and make them feel more connected to decision-making.

What worked less well: There was caution in the room that community organising might put unfair demands on citizens' time, and that it might put too great an onus on citizens rather than politicians to take the lead in effecting change. The Dragons also picked up on the idea that community organising would likely focus only on the 'smaller' issues where community action is guaranteed to have an impact (eg campaigning to keep post offices open).

The improved idea: Citizens argued that until the balance of power shifts – ie until more important decisions are made at a local rather than national level – an idea like community organising will have only limited potential to bring about real change. As such, to give the idea of localism and community organising greater legitimacy, and crucially, greater impact, citizens proposed the addition of local, issue-based referendums to decide policy and spending priorities.

Additional Dragons' idea: Stricter rules for MPs

The idea: Some citizens argued that the other pitched ideas ignored what we need to change most to improve politics: politicians themselves. They proposed as an alternative a stricter set of rules for MPs:

- MPs should only have one job, and give up any business connections on election
- MPs should be mandated to spend more time in their constituencies
- MPs should be made to be more transparent about salaries and expenses
- There should be fewer MPs overall

Conclusions: What does this tell us about how to re-engage people in politics?

To close our co-creative workshop, we exposed each of these citizen-proofed ideas to discussion and, ultimately, a (strictly non-scientific) vote. The citizen-improved version of 'giving power to local communities' won, with the crucial additions of secure funding to give the idea teeth and proper accountability.

However, the point of the project was not to find a 'silver bullet' for reducing the democratic deficit (although that would have been nice…) but instead to learn what needs to change to improve our politics. Here's what we learned, and what might be taken forward as a test for any future policy change:

Firstly, change must be rooted in an understanding of what *citizens* feel is wrong with politics, rather than a problem that only really concerns the Westminster elites. When asked what they'd most like to change about politics, almost every non-voter or swing voter in the room talked about changing politicians themselves: who they are, the way that they talk and act, and the kinds of issues they prioritise. For many citizens, a lack of trust in politicians not to abuse the system, and a belief that they don't understand the issues that matter to local communities, is an insurmountable barrier to feeling that they have any kind of control over decision-making. Strikingly, when none of the ideas pitched by the political campaigners and activists seemed to address this problem, citizens felt compelled to add in their own proposition – a stricter rulebook for MPs.

Change depends on politicians working much harder to engage with the people that they wish to serve. Rowenna Davis began her pitch for the original idea of decentralising power with a compelling story about a local campaign to stop planning permission going ahead on 'yet another' betting shop in Peckham. The Dragons, and particularly swing voters like Dionne, continually referred back to Rowenna's story over the course of the workshop, demonstrating the impact of an accessible, clearly thought-through narrative in capturing the electorate's imagination. Fabian polling corroborates this view: politicians seeming more like 'real human beings' comes second out of seven factors to improve politics.

Change should involve people, with the ultimate aim of making voters feel more connected to decision-making. Several citizens said at the start of the workshop that they see too few people 'like them' in politics, too little engagement between politicians and 'real' voters, and too little evidence that the public has any power to bring about change, even at a local level. Appetite to see people involved in politics and power put back in the hands of voters was also clearly reflected in citizens' amendments to the ideas pitched during the workshop, which included a proposal for a governing body or jury to oversee each MP, made up of a cross-section of constituents, and local referendums to decide priorities for national and local spending. **Importantly, these amendments also speak to a wider desire for greater accountability, and change that can be measured, not just talked about.**

However, swing voters and non-voters clearly feel that politicians should take the lead and have ultimate responsibility for change, rather than simply placing the onus on the citizen to get more involved. Over the course of the workshop, citizens tended to react against ideas that would put demands on their time without any clear outcome, and several reported demoralising experiences of trying to effect change locally without any success.

Symbols of engagement need to be felt at a local level before people will feel that they have a stake nationally. Two of the five final pitches, and the eventual winner, related to putting power back in the hands of local communities. The appetite to see the tangible effects of politics at a local level echoes previous Fabian polling which found that people would be most likely to vote in the next general election 'if people in political parties spent less time trying to win my vote and more time doing good work in my neighbourhood'.

Finally, although these typical voters and non-voters were disillusioned and sceptical, just one afternoon of deliberation demonstrated the potential for activating interest in politics when exposed to interesting ideas, engaging activists and by focussing on finding solutions rather than bemoaning problems. As Dionne put it: *"We need more things like this actually, just talking and thinking about things I never normally have time to think about."*

ESSAYS

At one point I thought I'd be on the stage, not in the audience. I'd started to run a selection campaign. The 100 or so members I spoke to liked my story about a more participatory politics, using the office of an MP to pull authority back from distant capitalists and bureaucrats and create institutions in our neighbourhood, backing community housing trusts, local banks, an energy coop. The members I listened to were some of my community's most engaged and active local citizens. Yet even they felt disillusioned and grumpy about the place of power in our polity and party. As the Fabian research this pamphlet introduces shows, a cross-section of the British public think decisions which affect them are made by people who can't be trusted and in institutions, whether business or the public sector, which are too distant from their lives. But, and this is the point, the *role* we ask politicians to perform is about wielding exactly the distant, dominating kind of power we don't like. It's a phantom kind of power that doesn't 'deliver' the outcomes it claims to. But we believe we have no choice but to vote for people who do things in a way we don't like. In my short campaign I didn't have the time or, perhaps the skill, to show how things could be different. So I withdrew, and supported the candidate who came the closest to what I'd been talking about.

Let's look for a moment at the role politicians occupy. On my way home recently, I opened the newspaper. In the *Evening Standard* for 18 March 2014, the main stories were Mr Trotter winning £108 million and the suicide of L'Wren Scott, both about the complicated, triumphant, tragic lives of real people. There were 11 stories about actual or possible actions by politicians. Five were about tax and tax credits, two about fines, one was about a big building project (HS2), one about whether UKIP would ban same sex-marriages, one about more funding for a public service, one about forcing public sector workers to report female genital mutilation. It was dry, boring and uncreative, with no mention of real people. Most importantly, the political stories were about very limited kinds of power. Politicians seem only to talk about money and force, about taxing, spending, compelling people to act in a particular way backed up by the state's threat of violence. What's distinctive about the kind of political action discussed in the *Evening Standard* – just like the stories candidates told in Woolwich – is that they do not require the consent or co-operation of the governed.

Our disillusionment with politics is caused by the fact that we expect more. Anger at politicians is a consequence of the massive gap between the promise of what politics could offer, and the extraordinarily limited way in which our political leaders talk about their actions. Politicians tap into this sense of what politics might be when they tell grand but vague stories about what they will achieve: 'a better tomorrow', 'a brighter future', even a modicum of economic prosperity. The popularity of phrases like 'we're all in this together' or 'one nation' shows that the public look to politicians to create and lead moments of common action. Political power, we believe, comes from what the Whig politician Edmund Burke (and then the philosopher Hannah Arendt) called 'action in concert', from people doing things together. We hope that politicians can create the situations in which we can collectively shape the destiny of our communities and country. But because they have such a limited and pessimistic view of the power at their disposal, because they imagine they can only do things with money and force, the public is continually disappointed when action doesn't match rhetoric.

My argument is that we, like the citizens of most other democratic societies, live in a polity where the language of our political leaders expresses an idea of power radically out of kilter with the way the rest of us think about political action. The difference is stark. It is about the relationship between freedom and politics. Freedom is a strangely underused word in our political language, but it is the idea that lies, hidden, at the centre of debates about political disillusionment.

Most politicians take what I'd call a Hobbesian view of politics and freedom. They imagine (when it comes to their national political role) that citizens give up a proportion of their freedom when they elect political leaders. People keep their freedom to run their private lives as they choose, but hand over their power to shape the place they live to politicians who, from then onwards until the next election, act without the consent or co-operation of those they rule.

Thomas Hobbes was a political thinker writing during the British Civil Wars of the 17th century. His writing was driven by an anxiety about what happens when people are free to organise and passionately impose their interpretation of the good society on others, which he thought led to death, destruction and lives which were "nasty, brutish and short". To prevent bloodshed, people needed to hand their power to collectively shape the society they lived in to a superior power that could act, with force, on their behalf, what he called the Leviathan. The legacy of that Leviathan stills lives with us in how politicians think of their own power.

Of course, there are still places where Hobbes' argument applies. We need to deprive criminals of their freedom. But for the most part we live in a radically un-Hobbesian world. Now, we live in a society where power is diffused in thousands of state and non-state institutions big and small: schools, hospitals, businesses, universities and countless others, which all come under some kind of political oversight. These institutions are populated by people who act from a mix of persuasion, example, reward, duty, friendship, loyalty and only occasionally force.

My argument here draws from the French philosopher Michel Foucault's analysis of the way power works in modern societies. Power, for Foucault, is not a scarce thing possessed by some people and wielded over others. It is always relational, always local. Its operation cannot be controlled by a single, distant, sovereign force. Foucault famously argued that we needed to 'cut off the king's head' in our thinking about politics. Instead of obsessing about centrally created laws signed by the Queen, we should think about the practical ways institutions work, the complicated relationships which make places like schools function. With their Hobbesian belief that power comes from their sovereign capacity to spend money or use force from the centre, our politicians have failed to keep up with modern times. Most important for Foucault is the idea that power is not the opposite of freedom. Power comes from directing the actions of people who, most of the time, imagine that they retain their freedom to shape their own individual and collective lives.

Take a school, for example. Where does power lie? What is it, in other words, that determines how a school works? Government establishes clear rules, the national curriculum and statutory guidelines, and has created the distant surveying presence of OFSTED. But how heads, teachers, parents and students respond to these distant powers is shaped by a thousand forces in the school itself: the quality of leadership, the way teachers have been trained, the school's design, the quality of relationships between staff and others, the social background of parents and students. Even amidst so many central rules, power operates by directing people who are free to act. Students are given incentives to behave, rather than being disciplined through violence. Teachers are 'guided' but not commanded in writing their lesson plans. Even the imperative to improve results is a choice. There is no law, and no violence that will follow, if a headteacher decides their school doesn't strive to be outstanding. There is an extraordinary amount of bureaucracy, and incredible pressure on teachers to act in a certain way. But what shapes how good the school is its culture and ethos, its social context, the quality of staff and leadership, a complicated mix of local forces.

Foucault's analysis, therefore, offers an important starting point to explain current disillusionment with politics. If power is dispersed and local, centred in the life of institutions we encounter everyday, in social systems and practices that can't be controlled by legislative force, it's hardly surprising we're turned off by politicians who believe central power can direct things it simply cannot control.

To end citizens' disillusionment with politics, we need to craft a different idea and practice of political power. That practice should begin by recognising the freedom of people, not simply to consume what we choose, but to collectively shape the places we live and work. The task of politicians is not to impose their will to achieve particular outcomes by force. Instead, it is to create situations where people can exercise their freedom to develop their own sense of the common good. That is the only basis for real power. It starts by recognising that free people have different interests. Teachers, parents and students, for example, do not necessarily want the same thing. The tension between them should not be suppressed. But the exercise of freedom involves negotiation. It is premised on the possibility of agreement, and on practices that encourage compromise and give and take.

Politicians should see themselves as creators not managers, as leaders who build and nurture institutions in which people negotiate and agree a common plan of action for mutual interest. In practice, that means considering many of the things Labour's policy review, led by Jon Cruddas, has started to talk about: local banks, community-controlled local housing, workers involved in the management of businesses, regional growth strategies in which businesses, unions and the public and voluntary sector work together, joint health and social care commissioning. In all these examples, the political role of creating a conversation that leads to common action and a jointly agreed plan is critical. The role of politics is not to act on behalf of a particular group of people (the poor, for example), but to ensure every interest has the power to make its voice heard within the negotiation.

Two attributes are needed for politicians to exercise this kind of power. First, to get people in the room by inspiring them with a sense of the possibility of common action. Secondly, the ability to chair the conversation, to ensure every interest is heard, to mediate between irreconcilable antagonisms and push discussion into agreement and action. All through it, the assumption is that politicians do not themselves make things happen. Their job is to enable the action of others which otherwise wouldn't have happened.

A politics of creative leadership needs to be translated into election-winning political rhetoric. Is that so difficult? No. But it needs three things. First, a clear and disciplined national message, which recognises what's wrong with politics and articulates a vision about people being involved together tackling Britain's challenges. Secondly, it needs a practical story about people having more of a say and stake in a number of important institutions: parents in schools, as Ed Miliband announced, workers on boards, power over economic regeneration with city councils. We might even have a pledge card outlining them. Third, it would point to practical examples of success, places where politicians have involved an initially sceptical, disillusioned public in common action. There are many of them.

The greatest challenge in overcoming political disillusionment is not language. It comes from the sensibility of our political leaders. It's usually different in their constituency, where they have strong relationships with local people and institutions. But MPs in Whitehall echo Thomas Hobbes' idea of political power because, to them, the world seems to echo a Hobbesian state of nature. It is full of competing interests which can't be trusted to work together well without force, inside as well as outside the Westminster village. Those interests make sure political life is often nasty, brutish and short. Human spontaneity is a dangerous force which needs to be blocked not channelled. Politicians try to govern with distant instruments that don't require the participation of the governed because it's the only way they imagine they can project an idea of their being in charge, amidst the chaotic demands of life outside Westminster.

It is, though, in the interests of politicians to change. In particular, this politics of creative leadership would allow politicians to escape their current state of feeling beleaguered by an infinite set of demands. Those are expressed as a demand for force to be applied on behalf of a particular interest: for rules to be written to fund some sector, to mandate public workers to act in a particular way, for some bad thing to be banned. Politicians feel besieged because they think they alone can decide, and imagine that when they act they can only act with force. Much of the time, in their day to day work, they don't think Westminster is the right place to make the decision. But they give in to pressure as we all assume Westminster is the only site of power.

The politician's response to those interests could be different: it could be to empower the voice of people within the conversation that shapes what happens in institutions that need to change. Let me give an example. There is an incessant demand from different groups for particular subjects to be emphasised in schools' national curriculum: citizenship, financial education, sex education, environmentalism, more that connects to work, more traditional learning, and so on. The demand is for politicians to use force to compel teachers to act, presumably against their will. The result is a crowded curriculum, and a diminishing sense that teachers have autonomy to develop their craft. The reality is that decisions are made by negotiation, but it happens behind closed doors because the myth the politician has sole power needs to be maintained. So when something is missed, citizens feel wronged and the pressure on politicians intensifies.

My argument is that politicians should take responsibility for creating the debate about what is taught in schools, not deciding every detail themselves. That might mean holding a convention, where teachers and parents, subject groups, campaigning organisations and business leaders discuss and agree what is taught in schools. The secretary of state still has responsibility, but it is to host not decide, to convene and chair a discussion, ensuring voices are recognised and those with less power are organised. Perhaps we decide a national curriculum isn't needed. Then the politician's job is to ensure different views have a voice in the discussion of what is taught in each school, again in public debate and argument, and again recognising that interests are not to be suppressed but be recognised as an integral part of the conversation that constitutes our polity. Anything other than that is the domination by distant acts of force, and it's no surprise people are turned off politics.

2 | THE PECULIAR CHARACTER OF POLITICAL SPEECH

Alan Finlayson

Political rhetoric is concerned with formulating and communicating an argument for a particular claim presented to a particular audience at a particular time. Unfortunately, a lot of political communication lacks an argument and this is why most people pay little attention to it. What's more, political strategists have over-promoted the character of leaders and parties, but without a specific audience in mind, politicians end up either presenting themselves as all things to all people or as nothing in particular. A prerequisite of turning around the reputation of politics and politicians is conviction – knowing what your position is, knowing how and why it is different from others' positions and being sure of why you hold it.

When the complete footage of a television interview with Ed Miliband appeared in June of 2011, it caused much mirth and confirmed many prejudices about the sterility of contemporary political speech. Asked a number of different questions about public sector strikes, Miliband simply repeated the same rehearsed response:

> "…These strikes are wrong, at a time when negotiations are still going on but parents and the public have been let down by both sides because the

government has acted in a reckless and provocative manner. After today's disruption, I urge both sides to put aside the rhetoric, get around the negotiating table and stop it happening again…At a time when negotiations are still going on, I do believe these strikes are wrong; and that's why I say, both sides, after today's disruption, get around the negotiating table put aside the rhetoric and sort the problem out because the public and parents have been let down by both sides, the government has acted in a reckless and provocative manner…What I say is the strikes are wrong when negotiations are still going on, but the government has acted in a reckless and provocative manner in the way it's gone about these issues after today's disruption, I urge both sides to get around the negotiating table, put aside the rhetoric and stop this kind of thing happening again…".

The video pulled back the curtain, exposing the backstage machinations characteristic of politics in a media culture. Miliband was playing the game as politicians and journalists understand it. Only a few seconds of an interview will make it into a broadcast package. Journalists want a clear quote that they can weave into the story they want to tell; politicians want to ensure that their message is the one that gets out.

But defences of Miliband which suggest that what he was doing was a normal part of political conduct fail to appreciate the extent to which political speech has become anything but normal. Miliband's interview was just one example of something very wrong. A YouGov poll in 2012 found that 62 per cent of us in Britain agree with the statement 'politicians tell lies all the time and you can't believe a word they say'. There are a lot of reasons for this. But the most important is that much of the time, politicians sound like liars.

What is political communication?

When political strategists think about promoting their parties' messages they are often minded to emphasise the 'communication' aspect of 'political communication'. They see their problem as one of making politics *communicable* – taking a body of ideology or policy and expressing it in ways that will be manageable, intelligible, and memorable. But what is it that makes something *political* communication?

The defining feature of politics is that, within it, *nothing* can be taken for granted. When scientists argue about the precise effects of climate change, they do so against a background not only of agreed facts but also of shared methodologies. As scientists, they agree on what a right answer looks like and on how to go about getting and verifying one. When scientists argue with climate change sceptics the facts are no longer agreed and there is no shared methodology. There is no agreement on how to frame the questions let alone on what agreeable answers would look like. It is no longer a scientific dispute but a *political* one. And it cannot be resolved by the participants alone. They don't even agree on what it is that is disputed. Resolution thus depends on some kind of third party: someone or something that judges the two sides and takes a decision. In democracies that third party is often (although not always) 'the public' or some part of it. Communication crafted in such contexts – where potentially everything is at issue and where our goal is not to convince an opponent but an audience judging between us – is *political* communication.

Political communication, then, is not reducible to talking points, soundbites and key messages, narratives, frames and brands. These may be part of political communication. But they are not fundamental to it. The essence of political communication – the thing that makes it what it is – is *argument*. An argument is *not* the claim you want to make.

It is the reasons you give to others for agreeing with and acting on that claim. If I say 'vote Labour' or 'scrap Trident' these are clear recommendations. They are not, in themselves, arguments. Nor is the political argument necessarily the same as my reasons for thinking these things. It is the reasons I present to others in order to motivate them.

Unfortunately, a lot of political communication lacks an argument. As a consequence, it is ephemeral. This is why most people pay little attention to it. Why would anyone want to listen to someone else merely enumerate their opinions? For that matter, what sort of person gets up in public just to state their opinions? And how much of a weird narcissist are they to think that we are being 'anti-social' or failing in civic duty if we don't pay attention to them doing this? If political communication in the UK is to avoid sounding empty, suspicious or indulgent then it has to have an argument.

The importance of rhetoric

The theory and practice of public argumentation is called 'rhetoric'. It's an old but much misunderstood art. Rhetoric is not language that is vague, verbose or manipulative. It is, as Aristotle famously put it, the ability to identify in any particular situation the available means of persuasion. The key terms here are 'persuasion' and 'particular'. Rhetoric is not simply about winning assent – that can be done in lots of ways including force, bribery and trickery. But these generate no depth of conviction and can mobilise no committed action. To persuade someone is to move them from one position to another; it is to provide proofs which change how people understand the decisions they are taking. However, rhetoric is not concerned with proofs that stand forever, with the unassailable grandeur of mathematics. Political decisions often invoke fundamental truths but the decisions themselves are always particular – they are about this election, this policy right now in this present situation. Political rhetoric, then, is concerned with formulating and communicating an argument or 'proof' for a particular claim presented to a particular audience at a particular time.

Classical rhetoric identified three main kinds of proof: the appeal to 'logos' – some kind of reasoning deduction; the appeal to 'pathos' – to the feelings and emotions of the audience'; the appeal to 'ethos' – the character and authority of the speaker. The best persuasive speech does not rest on just one of these. It weaves them together. The potentially rational claims one is making (the evidence and the deduction or induction which should follow) are in harmony with the emotional tone and underpinned by an apt 'character'. The first problem with a lot of the rhetoric in British politics is that it emphasises 'ethos' in a way that obscures the other appeals. The second problem is that it gets ethos horribly wrong. Consequently, where political speech should inspire confidence, trust and conviction it more often induces boredom, incredulity and contempt.

Characterising ethos

One of the roles of ethos in rhetoric is to establish a secure connection between participants, a kind of 'identification' between speaker and audience. This doesn't necessarily mean 'equality'. Plenty of people identify with political figures they imagine to be superior or more powerful than them. Sometimes this is because they want to feel protected and sometimes it is because the identification makes them feel more powerful. For this reason politicians may be concerned to look decisive, resolute and committed. Identification can also be based on a belief in overlapping interests – the feeling that someone wants the same sorts of things as we do. This is what politicians are trying to create when they show us they 'get it', that they appreciate the challenges 'ordinary people' face. Identification can also be based on a feeling of similarity. This is why politicians think they need to be seen doing 'ordinary' things; it's why Tony Blair spoke with glottal stops and why Nigel Farage always carries around a pint.

From the rhetorical point of view, the kind of identification you should try and achieve depends on the context: the issue at hand, the people you are communicating with and the argument you are making. It makes sense to demonstrate one's strength and resolution when doing so is part of a logical and emotional argument in support of a decision that will lead to challenging and difficult times. It makes rather less sense apart from that context. Yet something like this happens a lot. Under the influence of theories of marketing and branding (and as media concentrate ever more on celebrity) political strategists have over-promoted the ethos of leaders and parties. Ethos thus appears in politics untethered from particular audiences and issues. Without a specific audience in mind, politicians end up either presenting themselves as all things to all people (which seems mendacious) or as nothing in particular (as bland non-people). Even worse is that particular policy or other arguments, rather than be supported by a proof from ethos, become used as proofs of it. This makes politicians look untrustworthy.

Let's go back to Miliband. In his repetitive interview he made rather odd use of the personal pronoun. He says "I urge", "I do believe", "that's why I say", "what I say is". This verbal tic is not unique to Miliband. It is common to many politicians across the mainstream parties. Yet it is not a way in which the rest of us often speak. If you ask at the corner shop how much for a copy of the *Daily Mirror* the newsagent will say '55 pence'. They will not say 'What I say to you is, that this newspaper costs 55 pence'. Only a very strange person would say that. But notice what saying this does. It shifts the topic of the exchange from the price of the newspaper to the character of the newsagent – as if their telling you about the price is important evidence of something about them. Why would someone, we might think to ourselves, need to make everything into an argument about their good character? And we might reasonably conclude that it's because they have something to hide.

It's not entirely politicians' fault that they speak like this. It's partly a way of filling in time and airspace while thinking. Radio and television abhor silence and require participants to keep the flow of chat going in a way that is quite artificial compared to everyday speaking. It's also a result of the behaviour of too many political interviewers. The psychologist Peter Bull, who specialises in the micro-linguistics of political interviews, has shown in his article 'Slippery Politicians?' for *The Psychologist* that interviewers tend to ask 'communicative conflict' questions. These are questions to which all the possible answers are in some way potentially negative. One of Bull's examples is David Dimbleby asking Tony Blair, when he was prime minister, "Are you ashamed of British railways?" If Blair says 'yes' then he risks admitting to some kind of policy failure. If he says 'no' he risks seeming complacent. Consequently Blair equivocates. What else can he do? This example is especially interesting since it was part of a programme in which audience members also asked questions. They tended to ask 'why' and 'what' questions and as a result, Bull shows, more often than not got clear answers. In short, one reason politicians give stupid answers is because they are asked stupid questions.

Equivocation is not all that is happening here. If someone says 'this is wrong' then they are indeed saying it is wrong. But if someone says 'I say this is wrong' then they are not in fact saying 'it is wrong'. They are saying that they say it is. In the interview about the strikes Miliband was, as it were, standing aside from himself, and introducing himself to us as a third person. His words were no longer about the issue at hand but about him. He was telling us that what mattered most was not that the two sides return to negotiations but that he said they should. In effect he was saying 'look at me, being the kind of politician who says this kind of thing about this kind of issue'. One of the main causes of disaffection from politics is that so many involved in it cannot see just how weird this is while the rest of us can see it all too clearly.

George Lakoff's theory of 'framing' has become increasingly popular and influential in some political circles. His argument is that the particular words and phrases we use invoke much more general frameworks of thought. When the right talks about 'tax relief', for example, they invoke thoughts of something that is burdensome and activate a general frame within which government is conceived of as an unjust imposition. From the syntax of their sentences to the forced anecdotes they tell about meeting 'ordinary' people and the banal photo opportunities, politicians invoke a frame which indicates they think that politics is all about them. As if that weren't bad enough they then perform themselves badly. An old article of faith of screenwriters and other storytellers is that you should show and not tell. A character is established as heroic because they act heroically and not because everyone keeps saying that they are. But politicians have a habit of telling us what they should be showing us in a way that betrays their own lack of confidence in their persona, makes them seem suspicious and which communicates the message that they think of themselves as the most important issue of all.

Conclusion

The books piled high in the 'business' section of airport newsagents promise tricks, strategies and magic words that will work with anyone at any time. But there is no easy way to turn around the reputation of politics and politicians. Changing things will first require recognition of what is special about political communication: particular arguments in situations where there is no clarity as to what is the question and what an answer looks like. In that situation a prerequisite for being convincing is having conviction – knowing what your position is, knowing how and why it is different from the positions of others and being sure of why you hold it. You shouldn't change what you think just to please audiences – only how you say what you think. Secondly, political arguments are made not from one thing but several. They must be reasonable, invoke emotion and be articulated with a convincing character. Various pathologies of politics stem from overemphasising one of these. Thirdly, the reason, emotion and character you employ depend on the context. Politicians seem often to worry about inconsistency – but changing the ways in which you argue is not a problem if what you argue is consistent.

Finally, and perhaps paradoxically, if politicians want people to think better of them then they have to stop trying so hard. To be a great rhetorician, suggested Cicero in his work *On the Orator*, one has first to "master everything that is relevant to the practices of citizens and the ways humans behave: all that is connected with normal life, the functioning of the state, our social order, as well as the way people usually think, human nature and character". This is necessary in part because the political rhetorician has to be able to understand the different contexts in which they will find themselves and that requires having a good grasp of what it is to be one of the different kinds of citizens in the community. But it's also because, in the end, politics and the speech that goes with it exists because of and for that community. It is about, and it is judged, by them. The politician who forgets that may get away with it

3 | POLITICAL REFORM IN AN ERA OF ANTI-POLITICS

Katie Ghose

The way institutions are configured – their remit and rules – inevitably affects the style and conduct of the people who work within them. Banks are a recent example where the overall aims and regulatory framework are thought to have contributed to a risk-taking culture among individuals. Politics is no different. The right package of institutional reforms can help open the doors to a culture and style of politics – and politician – better able to engage the modern voter.

The growing disconnect between people and politics is well documented. We have the Hansard Society's annual *Audit of Political Engagement* detailing the problem and how it's getting worse. We have various other annual surveys of political engagement, including British Social Attitudes and Eurobarometer, all with their indicators pointing in a direction that threatens the legitimacy of our democracy. The IPPR recently highlighted turnout inequality, with poorer, younger people far less likely to vote than older, more affluent groups. We have sporadic but regular outbursts of media interest in the problem, most recently triggered by Russell Brand's high-profile call for voter abstention. And ongoing issues over MPs' pay, expenses and work outside parliament shore up the public perception of an out-of-touch political class 'out for themselves'.

As a result, it is now commonplace to cite voter disengagement as the defining problem of our political era. Less usual are practical, workable solutions. Brand's 'don't vote' mantra is an irresponsible and ultimately futile way of tackling our democratic problems. Influential though he is, Brand's call is unlikely to cause a break-out of mass non-participation sufficient to prompt politicians to radical action. More likely is that his voice will just drip further negativity into an already cynical culture and perhaps encourage already hardened non-voters to keep away from the polls. Voter disengagement is an incredibly complex problem and like all complex problems, there are no quick fixes.

Tony Wright, academic, former MP and chair of the 'Wright committee', which achieved significant reforms to parliamentary procedure following the expenses scandal, argues that only major changes to the make-up and behaviour of parliament will restore people's faith in politics.

> "... Structural reform is not the primary requirement if we want to tackle the expressed public discontent with politicians. Some reforms of this kind might be useful, but most are seen as irrelevant. The real discontent with politicians turns on how they behave, and the sort of people they increasingly are..."

Wright says that the way to re-engage the public is for politicians to change their behaviour, and for MPs to be drawn from a less narrow pool of candidates. He is absolutely right that these behavioural or cultural changes are needed, but he is wrong to think that structural changes are therefore unnecessary. Institutional or system-based reforms, like an elected House of Lords, a different voting system or further devolution may be "seen as irrelevant" by people with a deepening disgust for the political class.

It is also true that politicians may over claim the impact that political or constitutional reforms can have specifically on public trust. But the way institutions are configured – their remit and rules – inevitably affects the style and conduct of the people who work within them. Banks are a recent example where the overall aims and regulatory framework are thought to have contributed to a risk-taking culture among individuals. Politics is no different. The right package of institutional reforms can help open the doors to a culture and style of politics – and politician – better able to engage the modern voter.

First, a fair franchise for all citizens is long overdue and takes many forms. The experience of electoral reform in Scotland demonstrates clear benefits for citizens and parties. It shows that changing how we choose our representatives goes beyond the mechanics of vote-counting and seat allocation to affect voting and party behaviour. After two sets of Scottish local elections held under proportional representation (the single transferable vote), voter choice has more than doubled, uncontested seats are a thing of the past, and the one party states that used to plague Scotland have been undone. Changing the system has facilitated a change in culture. Reform has encouraged parties to alter the way they campaign and reject the notion of 'no-go areas'. When there is a value to second preferences, this shapes the tone of the campaign by giving candidates an incentive to knock on doors they would previously have ignored. Under this system, parties have less reason to strive endlessly for the middle ground, thus giving citizens more political choice. Political culture takes time to change, and bridges with disaffected voters cannot be rebuilt overnight, but the Scottish experience clearly shows that systems can be part of the solution.

Second, our registration and voting system should maximise the opportunities for participation. This means a 'registration revolution' to make sure electoral arrangements work for modern voters, from making it easier to register to making it simpler to go out and vote. We want to see same-day registration so that when interest in the election hits its peak (ie in the run-up to election day itself), no one is prevented from turning that interest into participation. Likewise, why not enable citizens to register to vote when they send in their council tax forms or apply for a driver's licence? Why not send young citizens registration forms when they receive their national insurance cards and involve schools too in helping them to register as part of their political education? This is the way to embed a new right for 16- and 17-year-olds (now Labour and Liberal Democrat policy) to vote within a wider programme of reform. Changing the structure of electoral administration won't change participation on its own – people need to feel that parties offer worthwhile choices. But given a lack of knowledge or confidence is increasingly offered as a reason for failing to turn out, measures to tackle this must help improve the situation. And let's address the culture of election day, which does little to inspire or engage. Democracy should be celebrated, so election day itself should be more of a celebration – perhaps a public holiday, or a rite of passage for first-time voters. Creating a culture in which voting matters and visibly so, can only help bring people back to the ballot box and make other forms of participation seem worthwhile

A critical aspect of changing how politics looks and feels is encouraging a wider range of people to pursue elected office. But if we cannot get sufficient numbers developing a voting habit – and appetite for other kinds of political participation – then the parties will continue to have a limited pool to draw from. Rule changes aren't the whole solution, but for younger generations put off by old fashioned systems, a registration revolution sends an important signal that our democracy is capable of renewal. 16 and 17 year olds are able to vote in the

Scottish referendum this year, and this provides another opportunity to assess the relationship between rules or systems and culture change. How will politicians, civic groups and younger voters themselves interact to shape the debate? And when the franchise is extended, as will likely follow in other UK public elections, will politicians give equal attention to the issues that concern young people as they do to pensioners?

Third, we must challenge the obvious structural inequalities in our democracy. Recently citizens have begun to question just who really runs Britain. As our big institutions from banks to the BBC have fallen into disrepute, people have quite rightly questioned how power is spread. We need to challenge the status quo and finish off, once and for all, the job of ensuring our second chamber is democratically chosen. Recent scandals in the House of Lords have reinforced the perception that our political class is completely out of touch with the rest of the country. Granted, elected MPs are no more popular than unelected peers. But the spectacle of entirely unaccountable peers such as Lord Hanningfield clocking in and clocking out to claim their expenses is a terrible blight on our democracy. House of Lords reform is a clear example of how institutional reform would dramatically alter the make-up – and size – of its intake with obvious potential to restore public faith in its legitimacy.

Fourth, we also need a cleaner, more transparent party funding system. Our recent polling showed that three-quarters of the public believe big money has too much influence on our political parties. Some 65 per cent believe party donors can effectively buy knighthoods and other honours, 61 per cent believe the system of party funding is corrupt and should be changed, and 67 per cent believe no one should be able to give more than £5,000 to a political party in any year. Perhaps most interestingly, more people support a state-funded party system than don't – by a margin of 23 points. It is high time that the parties get together and sort out this problem once and for all. With so many believing politicians give special favours to big donors, it is likely that the public will think well of any party bold enough to create a new, settlement especially if they are willing to sacrifice their own (party's) wealth in order to create a level playing field for others.

The relationship between structures and cultures works the other way round, too. What would happen if politicians were to heed Tony Wright's call to be "more straightforward, answering questions honestly, avoiding the routine point-scoring, not always traducing opponents, working together where they can, ditching the spin, acknowledging the complexities and limitations of policy making, telling the truth about problems, admitting they get things wrong"? One possible consequence is that this more authentic style of politics would encourage openness among the political class to discuss with citizens how to change the system to reflect the new culture. People want democracy to work much better, and whilst political reform measures aren't going to top voters' shopping lists when competing with pressing concerns about jobs, schools and hospitals, the need for politics to change is keenly felt. So electoral reform and a whole host of other structural measures could be put back on the table.

The number of citizens engaging in party politics is plummeting and it is creating a legitimacy crisis. The problem of political disengagement is too serious to rely on any single area of reform. Bringing our democracy back to health requires us to commit to a wide range of reforms that target both the structure of our politics and the culture of those participating. Our democracy also needs to better engage and involve citizens at all levels, and that means a stronger role for citizens' assemblies and other deliberative techniques that can amplify voters' voices outside election time and give greater impetus to voting too. When representative democracy fails to engage, deliberative and citizen-led participation can help bring people back into politics.

Ireland's constitutional convention shows how citizens and politicians can work together to deal with important reform issues. From the outset, the convention aimed to give equal standing to 66 citizens, (randomly selected and broadly representative of Irish society) and 33 parliamentarians, nominated by their respective political parties, overseen by an independent chair. It is one of many modern examples of deliberative democracy, where participants are expected to combine expert opinion with their own experiences and listen to one other before reaching their conclusions. The citizens' convention on electoral reform in British Columbia is another innovative example. It tasked 160 randomly selected citizens with the job of investigating options for electoral system change. Taking place over the course of a year, participants had the opportunity to learn about options, conduct town hall hearings with fellow citizens and for on-going discussion and deliberation. These and other experiments should stimulate us to consider how voting can be accompanied by numerous other possibilities for democratic participation outside election times. Politics does matter to people. The expected high turnout for the Scottish referendum shows just how motivated citizens are when the issue is immediate and their vote may impact the result.

Established democracies rarely see the sort of big bang moments that usually herald major constitutional change, but later this year the Scottish referendum offers us just such an opportunity. Whatever the result, the referendum leaves us with serious constitutional questions to answer. Whether to devolve more powers to the local level, what future for the House of Lords and how each nation's way of doing democracy relates to another's are just three issues that will need resolving. We need to seize this moment and use it to ask people what they want for the future of UK democracy. All parties should commit to a formal constitutional convention that places citizens and politicians round a table to give them equal voice in deciding the root and branch reforms that would bring our democracy into the 21st century. With the right processes in place to foster an open conversation with the widest possible range of voices, it would be a fantastic illustration of the fact that citizens and politicians can bridge the gulf and do politics differently – 'everyday democracy' in action. And perhaps a citizens' convention could finally do away with the false dichotomy between systemic change and cultural change. After all, bringing people and politicians together to build a better democracy demands that they act to achieve both at the same time.

4 | POWER SHIFT

David Lammy MP

As the political system has become ever more centralised, the human face of politics – the councillors, activists and mayors that people see and hear from most frequently – have less and less influence over the lives of the people they represent. To re-engage people and convince them that politics really can have a positive impact on their lives, we need to empower villages, towns, cities and regions to be able to determine what happens in their area.

Ask any MP, councillor or mayor up and down the country and they'll tell you the same thing: apathy and disenchantment with politics are rife. 'You're all the same', is a constant refrain heard by activists of all parties. 'You don't care about me', often follows.

We are witnessing a strongly-felt disconnection between the type of adversarial, centralised politics that people watch on the evening news or read in the morning papers, and the type of politics that they feel has a real impact on their lives. This misconception that politics no longer has any visible positive impact is a result of a great distance, both geographic and metaphorical, between local communities and the political institutions in which real power resides. The clamour of prime minister's questions and the pomp and ceremony of the Queen's Speech are felt to have little bearing on the single mum in Bolton who wants the streets made safer for her children, or the teacher in Derby fighting to keep the local library open. It is these local, single-issue campaigns that people are engaging with instead of national or even regional politics.

The problem of political disengagement stems, in large part, from a deficit of devolved political power and the diminution of local politicians' ability to influence events and outcomes.

The truth is that the British political system has, over the last half-century, become ever more centralised. As a result, the human face of politics – the councillors, activists and mayors that people see and hear from most frequently at a local level – have less and less influence over the lives of the people they represent. It is this emergence of a top-down, centralised political system that has led to a disconnect emerging across the UK between the public and their politicians.

Across the country, local communities are being deprived of the power to influence what happens in their area. In my constituency and many others, for example, the proliferation of betting shops is a major issue. The diversity and fabric of high streets, particularly in deprived areas, is being slowly eroded by a splurge of new betting shops, payday loan companies and pawnbrokers. Local people repeatedly ask why the council isn't doing more to control the proliferation and stop the local pub or post office being turned into a Paddy Power or a BetFred. The answer on most occasions is simply that they can't. The 2005 Gambling Act – one of the less well thought-through pieces of New Labour legislation – removed any real power that local authorities have to control the nature of their high streets and prevent them being taken over by betting shops. It is depressingly symbolic of what is happening in other policy areas, too. Local people demand action that their local representatives no longer have the ability to take. This quickly results in a sense of disenchantment and apathy – a feeling that, however strong local public opinion is, nothing is ever really going to change. Just one in four people now feel they have any influence over local decisions, with the figure closer to one in ten when it comes to national decision-making.

The lack of local power is an issue across the board. Take housing, for example. Local authorities are, on the whole, desperate to build more housing. Britain needs to build up to five million new homes by 2031, requiring a building rate far exceeding current levels. Today, over 400,000 households live in overcrowded conditions. Yet instead of giving local authorities real power to invest in their housing stock, a series of centrally-set restrictions limit the powers of local authorities to a barely manageable space. Budgets are being slashed too; by the end of this parliament, council budgets will have been cut by an average of 40 per cent. Local authorities find themselves starved of funds, deprived of power and unable to meet the demands of local people.

To begin to tackle this, Labour should commit to lifting the borrowing cap on local councils, giving more responsibility to control the housing stock in their area according to local needs. Only when local people see their politicians making a real positive change in the local area will they begin to re-engage with politics.

The cumbersome restrictions imposed by central government apply not only to local authorities but to devolved assemblies too. The Greater London Authority (GLA), elected by Londoners to run London in their interests, and the London mayor, who has the second largest personal democratic mandate in Europe (after the French President), still lack the powers to manage London according to the city's needs. Restrictions on borrowing, spending and taxation mean that the representatives Londoners elect to govern their city are severely confined by managerial, top-down bureaucracy flowing out of Westminster and Whitehall. Instead of being the governing body that London needs, responsible for city-wide planning and strategy, the GLA is, in reality, just another 'stakeholder' in the scramble for central government funds and attention. As a result, much-needed investment in London's infrastructure – such as Crossrail 2 and vital new Thames crossings – relies not on the decisions of London's leaders but on the whim of unelected officials. And on entire areas of policy – such as childcare or education – the mayor is barely able to influence what happens in the city they were elected to serve. More powers are slowly being devolved to City Hall, but at a rate that is far too slow and with a scope that is far too narrow.

Instead, the London Assembly should be given more fiscal power. London should be allowed to keep hold of the taxes it generates, and its leaders allowed to use that revenue to invest in the city. This is not a radical proposal. Rather, it but would simply bring our capital in line with its international competitors. London currently receives just 37 per cent of its revenue in the form of local taxes and charges, compared with an OECD city average of 55 per cent. It would allow London's leaders to govern the city without constantly needing approval from Whitehall departments, thereby reconnecting London representatives with the needs of their electors.

Across the board Labour should promise to implement a radical localism agenda. That cannot be a 'big society'-type of localism that forces local people to fill the gaps left by a rapidly withdrawing central state, but a co-ordinated shifting of power away from Westminster to town halls and council chambers around the country. Jon Cruddas has already hinted that this will be a core part of Labour's policy review, and we should expect to hear more about the devolution agenda in the coming months.

Importantly, this devolution should apply not just to the powers of local mayors and councillors but to the very nature of how our representatives are elected. A widespread system of primaries – in which local people are able to choose their parliamentary candidate – would achieve this. By giving local people the power to choose who their candidates are, instead of having candidate chosen for them by party headquarters, the public would be engaged in their political process from the very start. The act of helping to select a candidate is a much more powerful means of engagement than trying to encourage someone to support a candidate with whom they have no personal affinity or connection. Polls tell us that half of Brits want to be involved in their local decision-making. Primaries enable that.

What's more, primaries, by their very nature, force politicians to engage on a level that until now has been unnecessary. Candidates seeking selection could no longer solely canvass a small number of committee members or loyal activists in whose hands the final decision lies. Even focusing on party members alone would not be sufficient. Instead, they must seek to engage, inspire and mobilise a much broader section of the local electorate – from diehard Labour voters to ambivalent first time voters. That can only be a good thing.

In London, the Labour party must use its mayoral primary as a unique opportunity to meet, listen to and engage ordinary Londoners. This is a chance to get out around the city, speak to voters beyond Labour's traditional base and listen to what people want from their mayor and their government. If that chance is taken, the London primary has the potential to build a real Labour movement in the capital. It would be a movement consisting of people who, in selection processes decided by party insiders, are often ignored until much later on in the election cycle. Local communities must be engaged in the political process from the very beginning, not just the point at which the party HQ decides to allow them to have a say.

But all this means that the nature of our system needs to change. Labour's manifesto needs to include a real commitment to devolving power to local authorities and devolved assemblies. The initial steps made with devolution of power to Scotland, Wales, Northern Ireland and London were some of the biggest achievements of the New Labour governments. But we did not go far enough. To re-engage people and convince them that politics really can have a positive impact on their lives, we need to empower villages, towns, cities and regions to be able to determine what happens in their area. Only then will people once again see politics as a force for good in their community.

5 | HOPE AND FEAR

Jenny Andersson

Two trends are shaping European politics at present: the rise of inequality, which undermines the link between citizens and politics; and the rise of the radical right, which thrives when the mainstream left offers no alternative to austerity. European social democracy succeeds when it links utopian notions to practical reform. This is needed more than ever to show people politics has something to offer.

Recent municipal elections in France and the Netherlands have confirmed the writing on the wall for the upcoming European elections: the far right benefits where the left loses steam and where mainstream politics does not present the electorate with any alternative to austerity and inequality.

This doesn't mean the European left has lost all capacity to fight and win elections. After all, Francois Hollande won the 2012 presidential election in France, carried by a wave of optimism, which he rapidly squandered. Social democracy is highly likely to prevail this autumn in Sweden and Ed Miliband might well win next year in the UK too. But winning is not the same thing as wanting to change things, or convincing people the left has something important to say about the state of the world.

Europe is rapidly changing into a continent of difference. There are, in particular, two fundamental and interrelated trends that should worry us. The European continent has seen massive rises in inequality, trends that started long before the financial crisis but that took a long time to find political expression and raise reactions. As the French economist Thomas Piketty has shown (the success of his book *Capital in the Twenty-First Century* should be a real wakeup call for social democrats across Europe), inequalities with old historical roots have made a bold return in the last 30 years. They are not, as even social democrats claimed in the 1990s and early 2000s, an unhappy side effect of globalisation. They are to a large extent an active political creation, the result of policies which have increased incentives for individual advancement but reduced corrections for the effects. A number of factors have laid the basis for fundamental shifts in the distribution of resources in Europe during the neoliberal era: the rolling back of the welfare state, coinciding with increased unemployment following the deindustrialisation of Europe's manufacturing regions in the long period since the 1970s; the rapid growth of financial markets and changes in progressive tax systems benefitting capital gains and high incomes; the privatisation of housing markets and public companies. Even in a country like Sweden, inequality trends are taking extreme proportions, both at the lower and higher end of the spectrum, leaving an increasingly bewildered middle class.

Inequality is not 'merely' a problem of resources. Inequality affects the link between citizens and politics in a fundamental way, since most people feel that inequality is unjust and damaging to the society they live in. Inequality is also highly visible socially and has a great impact on people's lives and hopes. Inequality inspires fear, the feeling that life chances are controlled by factors far beyond ones own agency, and the fear that things won't get better in the future tends to lead not to political mobilisation but to other parties but actively making moves towards the centre of mainstream politics. This was clearly Marine Le Pen's strategy for the municipal elections in France and it is a strategy that we are seeing for the European elections too. This situation presents a fundamental moral imperative to European social democratic parties. The far right is very good at playing up people's fears. It is good also at targeting scapegoats, such as the Roma people abandoned on the streets of European capitals or Muslim minorities that are, in most cases, well integrated parts of our communities. Yet the far right does not have answers to the European crisis, and they do not know how to mobilise people's hopes. The European extreme right has a clear dystopia, but they are unable to present citizens with a vision for the good society and how politics can build it.

European social democracy, in particular the Nordic countries, has a historic legacy in linking utopian notions – for instance, the idea of the welfare state – to practical reform. More than ever, it is this idea of coupling a values-based social democratic project with a plan for action that is needed, to reinvest politics with the sense that even if change might not be quick and results immediate, at least there is a sense of direction. This must begin with a clear debate on the effects of austerity politics in further entrenching inequalities, and with an alternative platform for gradual investment in Europe's welfare states and re-forging the class solidarity that has been lost during the neoliberal era. But it needs also a much more vibrant political dialogue around these issues than is the case today. There is a tremendous project in not only restructuring but also explaining new tax policies that shift, a little bit, the burdens of austerity, of making the case for public education and other vital public services. The welfare state, identified for the last decades by European policymakers as a burden on the economy, needs to be rethought by social democrats as crucial for rebuilding the link between citizens and politics, for building new forms of class alliances and for articulating values of equality and solidarity.

While social democratic parties in EU member states are increasingly stuck in alliances, squeezed by electoral pressures and inhibited by internal fractions and power struggles, Europe is becoming a central political arena – both for a decisive debate on austerity and for a growing argument over how to forge a revitalised trans-European social democratic project. The European elections will most likely be a huge success for the far right. But they should be the occasion of a fundamental clash between nationalism on the one side, and a revitalised social democracy on the other. It is time that Brussels became the space for a discussion of what social democracy wants to mean for the world after the financial crisis and what it wants to achieve should it be granted a political mandate from the voters. The great sense of outrage that we are hearing has to be given a constructive direction, and social democracy is the only force in the political landscape that would be capable of providing answers to the immense economic and social challenges of a possible post-crisis world. This requires not only listening to European populations, but a new sense of political leadership.

polls indicate that the 2014 European parliament elections will see parties of the radical right and left increase their share of votes and seats, with an associated drop in support for both the centre-left and centre-right.

Academic research into this topic has tended to agree that people are showing growing signs of political disaffection. The most commonly observed trend is a decline in voter turnout, but also included is declining party membership, declining party identification, and declining trust of citizens in political institutions. In trying to understand these trends, the recent results of a YouGov poll conducted for *Fabian Review* suggested that one of the main reasons for non-voting was a disconnect between the culture of the popular classes and that of the political elite. Whilst not necessarily rejecting the notion that cultural differences are to blame for the lack of popular engagement with contemporary politics, most academic studies tend instead to focus on more long-term socio-economic and political explanations. These include developments which have reduced the scope for political choice and therefore rendered voting less important, including globalisation, lower economic growth and a neoliberal consensus. It also reflects changing expectations amongst an electorate that is no longer satisfied by a political system in which participation is limited to infrequent voting for political parties and their pre-formulated manifestos. Alongside these trends commentators also point out a parallel rise in 'innovative' forms of political participation, in which participation extends beyond the formal sphere of parliamentary politics. This includes petition-signing, attendance at demonstrations, as well as more direct action-type activities such as occupations, banner drops, blockades or media stunts. What observers tend to agree is that, whilst we might have witnessed a decline in popular trust in the political class, this does not necessarily reflect a wider disinterest in politics. The issue is with established channels of representation – and the fact that they do not appear to be doing their job of representation – leading to both a decline in voting and a rise in 'extra-parliamentary' forms of political participation.

The global economic crisis appears to have exacerbated these trends. Most obviously, this is the case with the *indignados* of southern Europe, large public demonstrations in squares such as that witnessed in Syntagma Square in Athens, the 'Uncut' movement in the UK, and the Occupy movement of the global north. What is perhaps novel about the post-2007/8 period, at least from the perspective of the formal sphere of politics, is the way in which these processes appear to have developed into a rise of protest votes and a polarisation of party systems. In the case of Greece, where these trends are perhaps most clearly evident, we see Syriza and Golden Dawn with a combined total of 89 seats (out of 300) in the most recent Greek general election in 2012. This is despite Syriza gaining only 14 seats in 2007, and Golden Dawn holding no seats at all. At the same time, the Greek centre-left party, PASOK, has seen its share of seats collapse – from 102 in 2007 (rising to 160 in 2009), to just 33 seats in the most recent 2012 election (the vote share dropped from 38 per cent to just 12 per cent). This is despite the fact that PASOK has been a clear natural party of office for much of the past four decades, being in government for 24 of the 33 years since 1981. Most of the predictions for the forthcoming European parliamentary elections indicate that these trends are likely to be seen across the EU, with a considerable fall in support likely for the centre-left and centre-right parties, alongside an unprecedented rise in the share of the votes for both the radical right and left.

How should political parties respond to each of these trends? How can parties re-engage with the electorate? Can we expect parties of the centre-left to re-connect with the electorate in such a way that a new, electable, progressive social coalition could be assembled?

Perhaps before we answer these questions we need to think in a little more depth about why these trends are happening. As already noted, this might be a question of the representative political elite having a detached political culture, but it would seem that this detachment exists for a reason. It may be that the electorate might be right in thinking that the political class have nothing else left to offer. Alongside globalisation and three decades of neoliberal ideology (which espouses the importance of 'letting the market decide'), there is an overwhelming sense that the governments of most advanced industrial democracies have now simply run out of financial options, other than reducing spending and imposing austerity measures. Faced with such a context, would it not make sense for the political elite to actively construct a culture of political disengagement, to ensure insulation from an increasingly mobilised and discontented society? We might expect the political elite to construct a common sense that 'there is no alternative' to balancing budgets.

Indeed, given that the political class routinely proclaim the importance of increased democratic and political engagement, it is remarkable how infrequently this translates into more concrete moves towards actively encouraging those new forms of political participation, as they emerge. This seems to suggest that there is a lack of genuine desire to see innovative forms of political engagement gather real momentum. See, for instance, the lack of any substantive political opposition by the Labour party leadership to the convictions of the UK Uncut protesters following their brief and peaceful occupation of Fortnum & Mason. The immediate reason for this lack of visible support for more genuine political engagement could have been the perception amongst the Labour party leadership that this would very quickly be tainted as 'radical' or 'returning to 1979' by the right-wing press. But it would also appear that most of the Labour party buys into the idea that there should be a more minimal form of democratic participation – hence the use of focus groups, targeting of the median voter, and distancing from the trade unions. This can perhaps in turn be explained in terms of the reduced range of feasible policy options created by the lack of economic growth and rising public debt – a context in which meeting more substantive demands would be too costly and therefore unachievable. In this context, a demobilised population might well be considered politically convenient.

We see similar trends in the views of the European political elite, and especially the centre-left political elite, regarding the European Union. It continues to be the case that decision-making authority is passed to the institutions of the European Union, despite its arcane and opaque nature, and the even greater levels of disconnection from the electorate than we see in national politics. Seemingly, the political elite would largely prefer to shift decision-making to the EU forum, because that is so much more isolated from political pressure than the national sphere – and in doing so it is easier to ensure that austerity and pro-market policies are the order of the day.

So, then, the more pertinent question than how can political parties respond might be: how can they respond *in a more progressive way*? How can they respond in a way that does not effectively constitute an attempt to silence and exclude?

Social democratic parties might look to Latin America for examples of experimentation by parties of the left. Here the most obvious differences to social democratic parties in Europe are the much more dynamic connection between parliamentary left parties and grassroots social movements. Whereas social democratic parties in Europe have lacked any meaningful engagement with many of the new social movements, and sometimes adopted a position of outright opposition to their natural allies such as the trade unions, Latin America's so-called 'pink tide' has instead witnessed innovative experiments in re-connecting the political elite with grassroots initiatives. In the process they are creating new experiments in 'radical social democracy' and reinventing the left and social democracy 'from below'. This is especially so in the case of Venezuela under Hugo Chávez, Bolivia under Evo Morales, and Ecuador under Rafael Correa. This has seen, for instance, innovative partnerships between social movements and parties of the left over water sector reforms. We have also seen in Venezuela under Chávez the development of *Consejos Comunales* that provided for a 'localised social democracy', in which, as Sara Motta writes, "the management and organisation of local community development are not undertaken by a technocratic or political elite but rather through a partnership between local community and state officials". Even in some of the more moderate social democratic governments that form part of the 'pink tide', moreover, we witness a strong connection between social movements and political parties. For instance, in Brazil the election of Lula's *Partido dos Trabalhadores* in 2002 was in part based on its relationship with the MST (Landless Workers' Movement), albeit a relationship that over time became more problematic as the PT sought to contain the more radical elements of the MST.

But this prompts a final question, of whether political elites want to reconnect with social movements in order to form a new progressive alliance? We often see social democratic parties act indifferently or even to repress new social movements that have mobilised across Europe in recent decades. This stands in contrast to the experiments in radical social democracy witnessed in Latin America, which as Steve Ellner points out, showed a willingness to support and seek out social conflict. This approach, says Ellner, resulted in radical social democratic candidates in each of these three countries winning referendums, elections and recall elections with sizable majorities (sometimes over 60 per cent). In contrast, recent research that I have conducted has highlighted how social democratic parties have been less than willing to embrace those innovative forms of social mobilisation and dissent that have emerged since the global economic crisis. In response to the occupation to prevent the closure of the Vestas environmentally-friendly wind turbine factory in 2009, for instance, the leadership of the Labour party made no public comment at all. Similarly, in response to the so-called 'Blockupy' protests focused on the European Central Bank in 2012, the German SPD issued only one reported statement, focusing on the banning of the protest and saying little on the actual claims being made by the protest movement.

If we are to see a more constructive engagement between newer social movements and social democratic parties across Europe, then we will also need to first see social democratic parties adopt a much more explicitly positive attitude towards contemporary expressions of dissent. That this does not appear, at least at present, to be forthcoming might be one of the problems. In short, parties need to let go and embrace the democratic energy outside of formal politics if they are to reconnect and beat the populist challenge. The question remains whether current party leaders feel either able or willing to enter into a process that is both more risky (as it would imply a loosening of their control of the party machine) and represent a dispersal of power away from the party leadership (and therefore represent the wilful ceding of power by those who have made a career out of accruing it). Alternatively, it might be more realistic to focus on attempts to directly build that democratic energy, as it develops outside of formal politics itself.

7| WHO HAS ABANDONED WHOM?

Ania Skrzypek-Claassens

Across Europe, politicians have put the problem of declining participation on the voters, rather than themselves, offering greater education or institutional reform as solutions. Instead, a new quality of European politics is needed to respond to voters who are ambivalent, not unengaged.

Everyone who votes does it for a reason. It may be rational or emotional; it may stem from family tradition or a sense of duty; it may reflect a desire to change something or to sustain the status quo; it may be self-interested or an expression of solidarity. Whatever it is, the person in question must have a clear motivation to get up, walk to the polling station and cast their vote.

Political science offers a great variety of explanations as to why citizens engage in this particular institutionalised political process. But in order to understand the dynamic of a specific election, it is not enough to analyse the motivation of those who cast their ballots. The reasons of those who have not participated are equally relevant, because it is their absence that ultimately threatens the legitimacy of the party with the largest number of votes. When low turnout makes the news, we speculate how far the result is representative of society, what shape the respective democracy is in, and how strong a mandate to govern the elected parties have.

Generally speaking, the same reflections accompany the results of European elections. There the turnout has declined rapidly since the first direct election in 1979, falling from 62 per cent to the alarmingly low level of 43 per cent in 2009. And though we try to console ourselves that these are 'second order' elections and therefore understandably attract fewer people to the polls, the implications are still serious. Low voter turnout offers additional arguments to those who claim that the European Union is undemocratic, or at best not democratic enough, as even its directly elected institutions do not enjoy trust and legitimacy.

However, our analysis of respective turnouts in national and European elections tends to rely on the narrative of the 'unaware voter'. This derives from both the 'baseline model' and the 'mobilisation model' of voting behaviour, whereby people are either too ignorant or too selfish to understand why voting in European elections should matter to them.

This has been an incredibly convenient explanation for both European and domestic politicians. It puts the problem of declining participation on the voters, rather than the political actors. Their excuses have remained technocratic: the uncompleted political union, an institutional setup that requires consensus, and the weak powers of the European parliament. And so their ways of dealing with the problem have focused on information campaigns, educational exchanges and school programmes. Even if these strategies had been successful in terms of raising awareness about the opportunities to engage, they do nothing to inspire that special drive citizens need to mobilise and take part.

Furthermore, the justification that 'people don't take part because they don't know' is simply no longer valid. We live in the era where voters are more informed than ever before, and the EU has become an integral part of national political debates in the aftermath of the 2008 global crisis. Hence trying to claim in June 2014 that the eventual low level of participation results from voters' ignorance, would be untrue, as well as irresponsible and offensive.

There is an alternative way of thinking about the problem of declining turnout in the European elections. This does not rely on an understanding of their specific character that makes them somehow independent from the wider political picture. On the contrary, it involves recognising that European elections will echo the tendencies observed in all elections. In short, the overall crisis of established politics, voters' disbelief in its power and subsequent resentment towards political elites (as observed during the wave of recent social mobilisations) will naturally resonate at a European level. Furthermore, because they are traditionally regarded as 'second-order' elections and so are seen by politicians and voters alike as kind of 'mid-terms', the tendencies to punish both the government and the strongest opposition parties may be even more apparent.

The reason why the latter tendency may be further stoked by European elections is that the competing parties tend to portray themselves as either pro- or anti-European. This is nowadays almost an archaic division, given that the complexity of EU policies means that a party can be for the integration process as such but stand in opposition to the contemporary policy directions of the EU. Nevertheless for campaigning reasons and the persistent assumption regarding voters' ignorance, the parties tend to simplify their messages. In the end, what citizens hear is whether the party considers the EU as important or as disruptive in terms of achieving its programmatic goals.

Additionally, while trying to 'bridge the gap' and 'bring Europe closer to the people', politicians try to be comprehensive and focus on topics they consider to be close to people's hearts. This is why, regardless of whether they are active on domestic or on international levels, they have a tendency to address issues primarily within the frame of their own state. For the European debate, this means talking about what a particular state loses or gains from their membership of the EU. These two combined – simplified pro-Europeanism and a restricted discourse about the EU – mean that the traditional parties easily enter the battleground comfortably inhabited by the anti-system, populist, nationalist parties. And this is how the latter ones get to dictate the terms of the campaign and frame the content of debates.

This puts the traditional and so-called pro-European parties in a defensive position. From that angle, they see the European elections as a challenge that requires them to first and foremost mobilise. Because of the assumed ignorance of voters on the one hand, and the awareness of continuously declining turnout on the other, they are ready to resort to unusual measures. That is why party lists include so many former officials and celebrities. Unfortunately, this actually has the opposite effect, further discrediting the process. Even if among these celebrities there are those who are ready to take the mandate seriously and serve to the best of their abilities, the vast majority are seen as ornaments.

It's important to stop confusing turnout with the level of awareness. It's also high time for politicians to become a bit more humble in terms of assuming that it's the voters' ignorance that prevents them going to the polls at European elections. On the contrary, they should look at the declining turnout as a measurement of the state of the politics they practise – and this should be the reference point for change.

This is about the quality of politics, not about institutional change. The solution to political disengagement with the European Union is not a new treaty. Even though the next stage of the Union's development may require a new framing, legal provisions should be seen as subsequent to a political vision which is yet to be formulated.

This is why it is so important that declining turnout is not misinterpreted as a simple incomprehension of the EU and its structures, but rather as a conscious choice of voters not to support simplistic pro-European standpoint. If we think about the decline of voters participation since 1979 till now not as one consequential trend, but rather a collection of indicators of what citizens thought of the united Europe at every respective given moment, we would have to say that the evolutionary drift on the wave of consultations and compromises is disappointing. A new quality of European politics is needed instead.

There are different benchmarks that one could imagine for this. First of all, it would require politicians to provide clear, ideologically underpinned alternatives. Rather than talking about upholding or dismantling Europe, they must define what sort of a question the EU should be an answer to nowadays. In the 1950s it was about ensuring peace and rebuilding the societies after the disaster of the wars, but this sense is no longer intrinsic. Instead of nostalgia, a new challenge needs to be identified, which a united Europe can successfully face and prove its present-day worth. Secondly, there would have to be a clear relation between these options and the shape that a new European social contract would take. Thirdly, we need to establish new patterns of political leadership, and a new sense of responsibility for European mandates. Hence the EU elections have to also become a moment of scrutiny. Fourthly, we must reinvest in deliberative democracy and include a European dimension. In that sense the role of non-governmental organisations is exceptionally relevant.

The challenges are immense, and the hopes of many are invested in the upcoming European elections. The Lisbon Treaty, whose provisions are going to be put into practice this time, is enabling europarties – the large groupings of similarly aligned parties in the European parliament – to campaign. There is therefore an expectation that there will be a greater convergence among the parties belonging to the same European political family – especially given they all nominated top candidates and adopted European manifestos. But although reaching this stage took a lot of effort, it should not be expected that a new bond with the European citizens will follow by a default.

On the contrary, regardless of this optimism-inducing historical achievement, the 'return of the voter' should not be taken for granted. The voters' disenchantment and resentment must be met with understanding, respect and readiness to discuss. It must be challenged with inspiring ideas and not with educational speeches on institutions. The new quality of politics must be about a politically distinctive vision, a readiness to humbly assume responsibility to serve, and about clear understanding of the politician-voter contract. The citizens may not instantly believe that European politics has become empowered and that politicians can swiftly change the world – but they have a right to know that those elected will respect them and that they will at least try.

8 | FOR THEM, NOT JUST FOR THEIR VOTE

Baroness Jan Royall

Turnout in European elections continues to fall and the democratic distance people feel from their European institutions is well established. Democratising Europe means making what if offers clearer, especially to Europe's youth. And it means engaging voters directly and finding out what they want, not trying to communicate with them through top-down messaging from a widely mistrusted political elite

Democratic engagement in Europe is worryingly low. Can we make a new case for Europe which will appeal to a new generation, and can the Party of European Socialists (PES) make it? The answer to both of these questions is yes, but we need to come to terms with the depth of the problem and put the young people of Europe at the heart of the solution.

The lack of turnout in European elections is alarming, even in countries that previously had a strong record of voting in them. In the Netherlands it dropped from 58 per cent in 1979 to 37 per cent in 2009. Average turnout across the whole of the EU in that period went from 62 per cent to 43 per cent. It is persistently below that of national elections, and even turnout in those is falling in many places. This malaise is affecting democratic engagement in general, not just the EU.

It would be a mistake to think that people have given up entirely on democracy, but the disconnection has deep roots. Many analyses focus on Europe's structures, and there are definitely areas in which reforms are necessary. But there is no single institutional reform that represents the solution to increasing engagement and that will re-energise democracy in the EU.

That is unfortunate for politicians across Europe, as the problem in fact lies much closer to home. Politics is viewed by many as a game played by a small elite, with the great majority of people neither able nor welcome to join in. This elitist perception is such that people begin to think – indeed, say – 'politics is not for people like me'; something compounded by the fact that many politicians don't sound or behave like normal human beings. It is a complaint I hear often while out campaigning and applies as much to Europe-wide politics as it does to any particular country's domestic scene.

The perception of an inaccessible clique is not helped by the fact that people obsessed by politics sometimes give the impression of spending their time only with people who are similarly obsessed. As Alex Smith wrote in late 2012, in *Total Politics* "the timidity and self-preservation in our politics stem in part from the fact that too few of those involved have lived anything like the experience of the British public at large... Outside of this bubble, the real world operates differently".

Community-based campaigning, talking to people about their own interests and building social connections is the key. The PES understand this, hence the great 'Knock the Vote' campaign being rolled out, in which young activists are listening to people's concerns as well as explaining our offer. The need for this kind of direct contact is heightened by the press in the UK, which is broadly speaking more than half eurosceptic. The success of this campaign will rest on making it clear that we are interested in the people we're contacting for them, and not just for their vote.

So instead of reconnecting people with politics, we have to reconnect politics with people, and this starts with our increasingly disaffected and disillusioned youth. I am leading the Labour party policy review into young people's engagement with politics and volunteering. As a result, I get to speak to many enthusiastic youngsters, but I also see the scale of the problem. Put simply, many just don't see politics as a force for good. A European Commission poll from last year showed, as you might expect, that fewer are participating in politics. Even so, I was surprised that 79 per cent wouldn't consider standing as an election candidate later in their lives.

It's no wonder they feel failed, and worry about the ability of politics to put things right. The essential inter-generational contract has been broken, the implicit post-war promise that each generation would ensure the next achieved a greater level of prosperity and security. Youth unemployment was too high even before the financial crisis, but the endemic waste of potential we see today is appalling. A recent report by the EU agency Eurofound illustrates the cost: 49 per cent of Europe's young adults live in a house with some level of deprivation, and more than one in five struggle to pay for basic needs. My generation, born into peace and prosperity, has failed in its responsibility. With the latest budget, together with hints about inheritance tax and the retention of universal benefits for the elderly, it is clear that the UK government is only concerned with garnering the support of the grey vote.

It would be too simplistic of course, to say that this failure has turned Europe's youth entirely off political expression. But it has changed the form that it often takes. Single issue campaigns are now often the vehicle; and in the UK we have seen how important this can be, with proper regulation of payday loan companies one cause that has been considerably advanced through such an avenue. It demonstrates to anyone that needs convincing that apathy about the world around them isn't the reason many youngsters have been turned off politics. As a recent report from the thinktank Demos illustrated, teenagers today care more not less about social issues, but they "do not rely on politicians and others to solve the world's problems, but instead roll up their sleeves and power up their laptop and smartphone to get things done through crowd-sourced collaboration". They also have a heightened sense of awareness of politicians who don't stick to their principles. Nick Clegg's well documented about turn on tuition fees has seemingly confirmed the worst suspicions of many, and made it far more difficult to put across the wider case for politics as a positive force.

How then to persuade Europe's youth that there's a point to politics, at both a national and European level? It's not through a managerial timidity; and certainly not through using excessively bureaucratic Euro-speak rather than talking normally. It's through a radical honesty, based on not making promises you can't keep but ones you can exceed.

Progressive and practical policies, such as guaranteeing jobs for Europe's young people are a good start. In the UK, Labour has put this at the centre of our offer, as have the PES. This is crucial because some polls show that, despite ambivalence towards the EU as a whole, many people are pretty sympathetic to what it actually does. A Fabian Society poll from 2010 is a good example. 45 per cent of respondents said membership of the EU was a bad thing for Britain, compared with 22 per cent who thought it was a good thing. However, a majority wanted EU countries to work closer on regulating financial institutions and protecting workers rights. Presumably, if the link between the mechanism of the EU and the offer were clearer, then people would look upon it more favourably.

Nevertheless, it is hard to make the right offer at a European level when you're not in the majority. And it may become even more difficult this year if the European Parliament is made near unworkable by the rise of inward looking groups with neither the inclination nor ability to see Europe's democratic institutions work for the people of Europe. Beppe Grillo and Nigel Farage's blends of populism share little, but together they threaten to bring it all to a grinding halt.

The challenge is great. But so is the prize, because young people across the EU who have grown up with it see the benefits through simple things like budget airline flights to places that previous generations would have found considerably more difficult to reach. Timothy Garton Ash points out that those benefits are fortunately taken for granted:

> *"The fact that a young man in Greece or Estonia can get on a plane in the morning and fly to Paris or Rome, without border controls and without exchanging money, and perhaps find a wife or friends there, decide to live or find a job there – this is progress that no one should put at risk. It must be made clear to people that their 'easyJet Europe', as I call this European freedom we experience every day, will be in jeopardy if the eurozone falls apart".*

So democratising Europe means making what it offers clearer, especially to Europe's youth. It means connecting the benefits to the institutions that make it function, and fighting the rise of extremists that endanger it. And it means engaging voters directly and finding out what they want, not trying to communicate with them through top-down messaging from a widely mistrusted political elite. I'm confident that both Labour and the PES can do that across Europe, in 2014 and beyond.

Discussion Guide: Back to Earth

How to use this Discussion Guide

The guide can be used in various ways by Fabian Local Societies, local political party meetings and trade union branches, student societies, NGOs and other groups.

- You might hold a discussion among local members or invite a guest speaker – for example, an MP, academic or local practitioner to lead a group discussion.

- Some different key themes are suggested. You might choose to spend 15–20 minutes on each area, or decide to focus the whole discussion on one of the issues for a more detailed discussion.

A discussion could address some or all of the following questions:

1. Is there a problem with the culture of politics? Can our current politicians close the gap between the political class and the people or do we need new politicians?

2. Decentralisation and giving power to communities was cited by our research as a key way to restore people's trust in politics. How far is this practicable? What are the limitations of this approach and how can the next Labour government give power away in a way that doesn't exacerbate existing spatial inequalities?

3. The citizens taking part emphasised "a wider desire for greater accountability, and change that can be measured, not just talked about". How can more dispersed political power still be accountable? Are our existing institutions of local and community engagement "fit for purpose" or do we need new institutions?

Please let us know what you think

Whatever view you take of the issues, we would very much like to hear about your discussion. Please send us a summary of your debate (perhaps 300 words) to debate@fabians.org.uk.

Queries

▬▬▬ THE EUROPEAN PROGRESSIVE MAGAZINE ▬▬▬

FACING
DEMOCRATIC MALAISE
A challenge for a political union

THINK EUROPEAN
Read European

SUBSCRIBE AT
WWW.QUERIES-FEPS.EU

FOUNDATION FOR EUROPEAN
PROGRESSIVE STUDIES
FONDATION EUROPÉENNE
D'ÉTUDES PROGRESSISTES

FOR A NEW SOCIAL DEAL

"Next Left: For a New Social Deal" presents a new way of thinking about the relations that should be forged between the world of fi nancial capitalism and politics, so that the path can be paved towards a better, fairer society. Deriving from previous deliberations on the modern understanding of progressive values, the FEPS Next Left Focus Group Members take herewith a challenge to seek their translation into a new narrative. The objective is therefore to reach beyond the crisis-induced confi nement of politics, and while stretching the borders of political imagination point at new horizons of a historical mission for social democracy.

The **"Next Left: For a New Social Deal"** is 6th volume of the FEPS Next Left Book Series. It is composed of 3 Chapters: **"Shaping A New Social Contract", "Ensuring Fair Distribution of Income, Wealth and Power"** and **"Building Progressive Alliances"**. It illustrates the outcomes of the work of the FEPS Next Left Focus Group within the year 2012, which herewith is being presented for consideration of the progressive movement.

FEATURING: Rémi BAZILLIER, Andrius BIELSKIS, Patrick DIAMOND, Karl DUFFEK, Alfred GUSENBAUER, John HALPIN, Ania SKRZYPEK, Ernst STETTER, Dimintris TSAROUHAS, Ignacio URQUIZU.

IN THE NAME OF POLITICAL UNION

"In the Name of Political Union – Europarties on the Rise" is the 7th volume of the FEPS Next Left Book series. Being at the same time the fi rst publication of the FEPS Next Left Working Group on europarties and eurodemocracy, this collection invites to explore a new avenue of research within the exciting journey towards the renewal of social democracy. It leads through questions regarding potential for politicisation and democratisation of the European Union, which queries come particularly timely taking into account 20th anniversary of the Treaty of Maastricht.

"In the Name of Political Union: Europarties on the Rise" constitutes a great collection of analyses, which paint an accurate panorama of political and partisan landscape on the European level. Thanks to this interdisciplinary and pan-European character they make a strong case that there is a potential for further development of the europarties and that the progressive family has a full potential to make the upcoming elections historical ones indeed.

FEATURING: Rémi BAZILLIER, Andrius BIELSKIS, Patrick DIAMOND, Karl DUFFEK, Alfred GUSENBAUER, John HALPIN, Ania SKRZYPEK, Ernst STETTER, Dimintris TSAROUHAS, Ignacio URQUIZU.

JOIN
BRITAIN'S ONLY
MEMBERSHIP
THINK TANK

Members of the Fabian Society receive at least four pamphlets or books a year as well as our quarterly magazine, 'Fabian Review'. You'll also receive invitations to special members' events and regular lectures and debates with leading politicians and thinkers.

For just £3.50 a month you can join now and we'll send you two pamphlets and the latest magazine free.

Call 020 7227 4900, email us at info@fabian-society.org.uk, or go to www.fabians.org.uk for more information

One Nation in the World

A new foreign policy for the left

Edited by
Marcus Roberts
and Ulrich Storck

The world has changed dramatically since Labour last won power in 1997. While Labour has been has been gradually assembling domestic policy ideas under its 'one nation' banner, the party has not yet managed to find a compelling voice on global issues.

To present himself as a credible prime minister in waiting, Ed Miliband will need to craft a story which makes sense of the world in which he will govern, as well as an aspirational account of what a Labour government might seek to do. This collection of essays explores the choices, strategy and values that can guide the next Labour government as it seeks to addresses the challenges of a new global agenda.

With chapters by Olaf Boehnke, Ian Bond, Rachel Briggs, Malcolm Chalmers, David Clark, Rachael Jolley, Mark Leonard, Jessica Toale and Duncan Weldon.

Within Reach

The new politics
of multiple needs
and exclusions

Edited by
Ed Wallis and
Oliver Hilbery

Across the country there is a small group of people who face multiple problems such as homelessness, substance misuse, mental health problems and offending. They slip between the cracks of mainstream public services and they fall out of a political debate that is unrelentingly focused on majoritarian concerns.

As we approach 2015, politicians from all parties are beginning to define the ideas that will shape our public services for the future. But what does this thinking really mean for those facing multiple needs and exclusions?

In Within Reach: The new politics of multiple needs and exclusions, politicians and policy experts from across the political spectrum outline how our services need to change to provide the kind of support the most vulnerable in our society really need.